THE UNIVERSE

Saturn

Tim Goss

www.heinemann.co.uk/library
Visit our website to find out more information about Heinemann Library books.

To order:
 Phone 44 (0) 1865 888066
 Send a fax to 44 (0) 1865 314091
Visit the Heinemann Bookshop at www.heinemann.co.uk/library to browse our catalogue and order online.

First published in Great Britain by Heinemann, Halley Court, Jordan Hill, Oxford, OX2 8EJ, part of Pearson Education.
Heinemann is a registered trademark of Pearson Education Ltd.

Editorial: Nick Hunter and Rachel Howells
Design: Richard Parker and Tinstar Design
Illustrations: Art Construction
Picture Research: Mica Brancic
Production: Julie Carter

Originated by Modern Age
Printed and bound in China by Leo Paper Group

ISBN 9780431154749 (hardback)
11 10 09 08 07
10 9 8 7 6 5 4 3 2 1

ISBN 9780431154879 (paperback)
12 11 10 09 08
10 9 8 7 6 5 4 3 2 1

British Library Cataloguing in Publication Data
Goss, Tim
Saturn. - (The universe)
523.4'6

A full catalogue record for this book is available from the British Library.

Acknowledgements
The Publishers would like to thank the following for permission to reproduce photographs: p. 4 NASA/Ames Research Center; pp. 5T, 24 NASA/Ames Research Center/Rick Guidice; p. 5B Vince Sterano/Corbis; p. 6 D. Van Ravenswaay/Photo Researchers, Inc.; pp. 7, 8, 11, 12, 14, 16, 17, 18, 20B, 21, 25, 26, 28, 29 NASA/JPL/Caltech; p. 9 Phil Nicholson/Cornell University, Steve Larson/University of Arizona, and NASA; p. 10 Erich Karkoschka/University of Arizona Lunar & Planetary Lab and NASA; p. 13 Reta Beebe/New Mexico State University, D. Gilmore and L. Bergeron/Space Telescope Science Institute, and NASA; p. 15 NASA/JPL/Caltech/National Space Science Data Center; p. 19 Science Photo Library/NASA; p. 20T NASA/U.S. Geological Survey; pp. 22, 23 Courtesy of Calvin J. Hamilton/www.solarviews.com, p. 27 NASA/JPL/Space Science Institute

Cover photograph reproduced with permission of ESA/University of Colorado, LASP.

The publishers would like to thank Geza Gyuk of the Adler Planetarium, Chicago, for his assistance in the preparation of this book.

Every effort has been made to contact copyright holders of any material reproduced in this book. Any omissions will be rectified in subsequent printings if notice is given to the publishers.

Contents

Any words appearing in the text in bold, **like this**, are explained in the glossary.

Where in the sky is Saturn?

On a clear night, when the **stars** are shining brightly, you might see one star that does not twinkle. If you do, you are not looking at a star. You may be looking at the **planet** Saturn. Saturn is the sixth planet from the Sun in our **solar system**.

Saturn is the second largest planet. Only Jupiter is larger than Saturn. If Saturn were hollow, you could fit 760 Earths inside of it. With a **telescope**, you can see the rings around Saturn and even some of the planet's **moons**.

This image shows the true colour of Saturn. It is a combination of two pictures of the planet.

The solar system

The solar system is made of all the planets, **comets**, and **asteroids** that circle the Sun. The Sun's **gravity** pulls on all of the objects in our solar system. If it were not for the pull of the Sun, the planets would travel in straight lines. This would send them out into deep space! The force of gravity keeps the planets in regular paths around the Sun called **orbits**.

Who found Saturn?

People have been looking at Saturn for a long time, since prehistoric times. They were able to do so because you can see the planet without a telescope. They did not know for sure what they were looking at, though. In 1610, the famous Italian **astronomer** Galileo Galilei used an early telescope and saw the planet more closely. He noticed the rings, but the image was fuzzy and the rings looked like "handles" on the planet or perhaps moons next to it. Dutch scientist Christiaan Huygens used a better telescope in 1655 and worked out a few years later that the "handles" around Saturn were actually rings.

Saturn is the sixth planet from the Sun.

How did Saturn get its name?

The name Saturn comes from the Latin name Saturnus. Saturnus was the Roman god of seeds, planting, and farming. People usually honoured him at harvest festivals. In Rome, the capital of Italy, you can still see what is left of a temple built to honour Saturnus.

How does Saturn move through space?

Saturn is the sixth **planet** from the Sun. It is ten times further from the Sun than Earth, so Saturn has to travel a much longer path to loop once around the Sun. This loop around the Sun is called a planet's **orbit**. The time it takes for a planet to make one orbit is called a **year**. Earth's year is 365 **days** long. Saturn's year is 29.5 times as long as an Earth year. This is because Saturn has further to go and moves more slowly than Earth.

Saturn moves more slowly than Earth in its orbit, because the force of the Sun's **gravity** is weaker further out.

We have day and night on Earth because Earth spins as it **revolves** around the Sun. Sometimes we are facing the Sun and it is day. When it is night, the part of the Earth we live on is facing away from the Sun. An Earth day is 24 hours long. Saturn spins much faster than Earth. A day on Saturn lasts only about 10.5 hours.

What are Saturn's rings made of?

Before there were powerful **telescopes** and **space probes**, people thought that Saturn had one ring. They thought the ring was a single, solid object. As early as 1660, a scientist called Jean Chapelain suggested that the rings were made of many small objects. Since almost everyone was convinced that the ring was solid, they ignored Chapelain. Almost 200 years passed before James Clerk Maxwell's studies showed that the rings were made of more particles than anyone could count.

Today we know that Saturn's rings are made of frozen water (ice), dust, and perhaps some bits of rock. Pieces of ice in Saturn's rings can be smaller than your hand, or as long as a bus. The chunks form a ring when they travel close together in orbits around Saturn. The rings reflect a lot of light because they are made mostly of ice.

The different colours in this image represent possible differences in the chemicals found in the rings of Saturn.

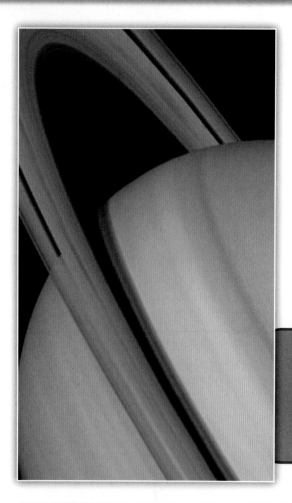

How did Saturn get its rings?

Scientists are not sure where the chunks in Saturn's rings came from. They may have formed after Saturn became a **planet**. They might be small pieces from ancient **moons** that were broken when **comets** or **meteorites** crashed into them.

Saturn has four main ring groups and three more faint, narrow groups with gaps in between them.

Cassini's Gap

In 1675, the French **astronomer** Giovanni Cassini found a dark area in Saturn's "ring". He later discovered that the dark area was really a hole or a gap. This meant that Saturn had at least two separate rings. Cassini's Gap is there because ring particles that **orbit** at that distance from the planet get thrown out of orbit. This happens because the particles in that section are repeatedly pulled on by the moons of Saturn. Today we know that the gap is not completely empty. It contains at least 100 smaller rings called **ringlets**.

What's special about Saturn?

Saturn could float in water. Even though it is so huge, if you could put Saturn in an ocean – it would float. That is because Saturn has the lowest **density** of all the planets. Density is a comparison of how much stuff an object is made of to how much space it takes up. A ball of cotton is less dense than a rock of the same size. Earth is much smaller than Saturn, but it has a much greater density.

Sometimes the rings disappear

In 1612, two years after Galileo first saw the rings of Saturn, he looked again and saw that the "handles" had disappeared. In later observations, he saw the rings again. Dutch scientist Huygens studied Saturn's rings and predicted that in the summer of 1671 they would again "disappear". He was right. Where did they go?

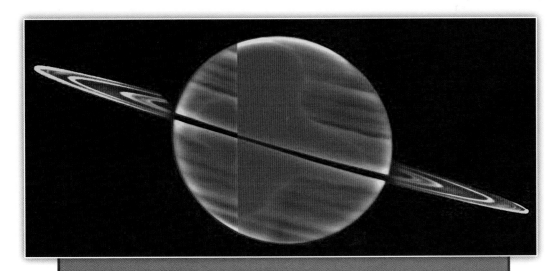

This infrared picture of Saturn shows almost the edge of the rings.

Travelling on a tilt

Saturn moves through space on a tilted **axis**, just like Earth does. This means that scientists usually see the rings at an angle. They see part of the top or the bottom of the rings. Huygens discovered that every 14 or 15 years, Earth passes through the plane of Saturn's rings. At this time scientists on Earth see only the edge of the rings. It is called a **ring-plane crossing**.

The rings are from 10 metres (33 feet) to 100 metres (328 feet) thick. Across a distance of millions of kilometres of space, it is hard to see something that narrow, even with a **telescope**. The glare from the rings almost disappears with an edge-on view. It looks like the rings are not there.

Without the rings reflecting sunlight, it is easier to see the **moons**. In this edge-on view of Saturn, you can see five of the planet's moons and the shadow of another.

How's the weather on Saturn?

If you ever plan a trip to Saturn, you had better have a very warm space suit. Temperatures in Saturn's **atmosphere** can get as low as –176°C (–285°F). That is more than twice as cold as the coldest temperatures on Earth.

Strong winds on Saturn push the cloud layers around the **planet** at very high speeds. **Space probes** have measured wind on Saturn moving at speeds faster than 1,770 kilometres (1,100 miles) per hour). This is about four times as fast as the quickest racing cars on Earth.

Every day's weather report: windy and cloudy

The winds blow every **day** on Saturn. The planet is always covered with clouds. Earth's clouds usually look white because they contain mostly water droplets and ice crystals made of water. Saturn's clouds appear yellow, red, and brown. The yellow comes from the ammonia crystals that cause the clouds to form. When other elements, such as phosphorus, also get into Saturn's clouds, they cause other colours to appear.

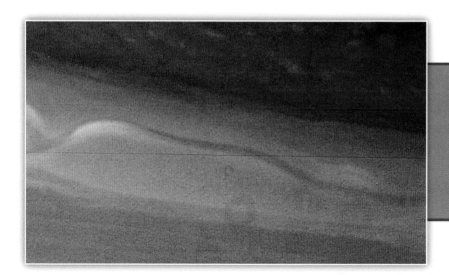

In this image of Saturn's atmosphere, a wave in the clouds is visible.

Do you like stormy weather?

About every 30 Earth **years**, there is a huge storm on Saturn that lasts about a month. This storm is called the Great White Spot. The clouds in this storm are very bright. You can see them with a **telescope** from your own garden. As the storm comes to an end, the spot stretches out into a white stripe across the **planet**.

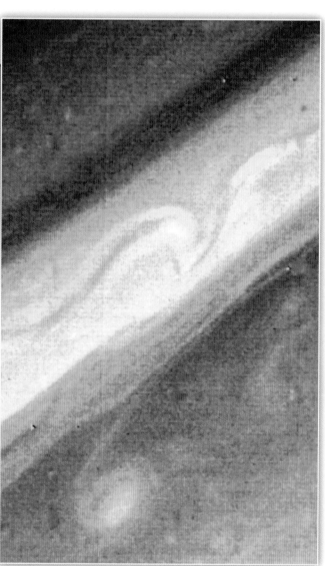

Winds have made a shape like the number "6" in the lower left corner of this image.

There are other storms that happen on Saturn, too. Some of them cover an area as large as the diameter of Earth. During storms on Saturn, lightning often flashes from cloud to cloud.

Why is Saturn so cold?

Saturn only receives about one per cent of the amount of sunlight that Earth does. This is because Saturn is almost ten times further away from the Sun. This can only warm the planet a little bit. In fact, Saturn gives off about twice as much heat as it receives from the Sun. The heat given off by the planet mostly comes from its **core**.

When Saturn first formed, much of the planet's heat was trapped in its **atmosphere** and core. Saturn has slowly been losing that heat ever since. Today the temperature of Saturn's outer layer is about –170°C (–274°F).

The white feature just above the rings, near the planet's **equator**, is a storm.

What would I see if I went to Saturn?

After travelling through the darkness of outer space, you would see Saturn glowing golden as you approached. The mystery of Saturn's golden glow was not solved until the National Aeronautics and Space Administration (NASA) sent **space probes** to the ringed **planet**.

Thick layers of clouds cover Saturn. NASA's probes provided information about the types of gas in the **atmosphere** of Saturn that give these clouds their colour. Light rays from the Sun strike the clouds and make them shine brightly.

A light show

The combination of **solar wind** and Saturn's magnetic field causes Saturn to have **auroras** at its poles. Stray particles from the Sun are pulled in by the magnetic field and crash together, giving off energy in the form of light. This makes the sky fill with blues, reds, and greens in wavy patterns. An aurora on Saturn is like the northern lights on Earth, only much brighter.

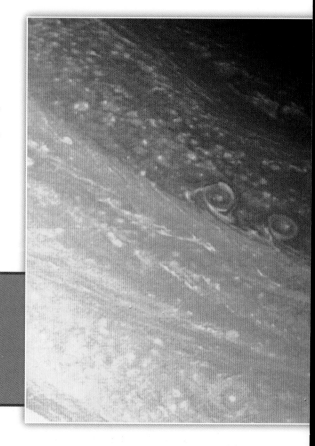

The bands you see in pictures of Saturn are bands of clouds moving rapidly around the planet. Each band moves at a slightly different speed.

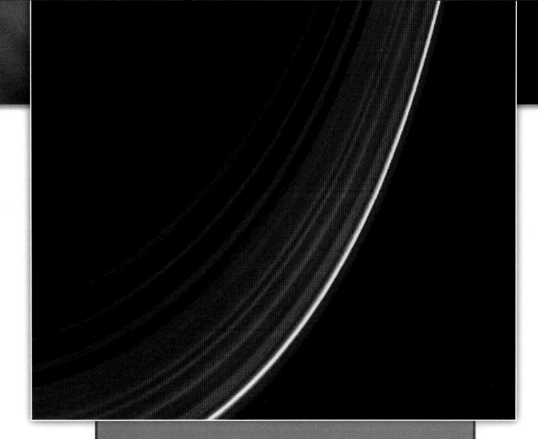

Close-up photographs of Saturn's rings like this one help scientists to study them more easily.

A bumpy ride

Flying through the rings would be a bumpy ride because of all the lumps of ice that would bang into your spacecraft. Saturn also has a very strong magnetic field around it and high levels of radiation. The magnetic field traps charged particles from the Sun, which creates the radiation.

Floating through the atmosphere

Once you got through the magnetic field, you would enter the atmosphere. Most of Saturn's atmosphere is made of hydrogen gas. Saturn's atmosphere has more hydrogen than any planet. Some of the hydrogen is combined with other chemicals. The rest of the atmosphere is mostly helium gas. Helium is used here on Earth to make balloons float in the air.

Saturn's cloud layers

The **atmosphere** of Saturn has three thick layers of clouds. When you look at Saturn through a **telescope** or at a picture from a **space probe**, the "surface" that you see is really the cloud layers that cover the **planet**. The outer cloud layers are about 400 kilometres (250 miles) deep.

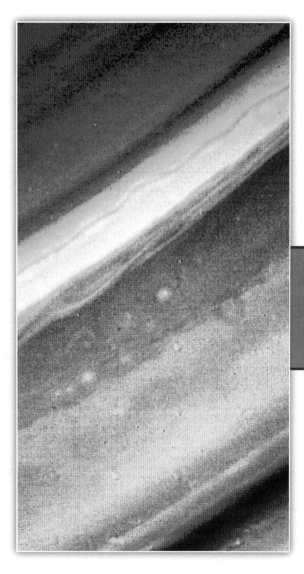

Each of Saturn's three cloud layers is different. The top cloud layer is made of ammonia crystals. Frozen ammonia crystals look like tiny pieces of hail. They float in the clouds high up in the atmosphere of Saturn.

Different colours help us to see the different cloud layers near Saturn's northern polar region.

Ammonia gas freezes into crystals because the temperatures in this layer are much colder than those in the cloud layers deeper inside Saturn. The top cloud layer looks pale and creamy.

The middle cloud layer of Saturn is made of a different type of ammonia crystal mixed with hydrogen and **sulphur**. This layer is red and brown.

The bottom cloud layer is a hazy colour of greyish blue. It is made of frozen water crystals and ammonia droplets. Earth's clouds have water droplets that we call rain.

Scientists do not know what the atmosphere is like below the bottom cloud layer. Future space probes may answer this question.

No ground to stand on

Saturn does not have a surface. The atmosphere simply gets thicker and thicker until it is a liquid. Scientists do not think there is any water in this layer of Saturn.

The colours in this image were adjusted to make Saturn's surface easier to see.

Many, many moons

If you like looking at Earth's **Moon**, you could have a lot of fun on Saturn. As you fly through the upper **atmosphere** of Saturn you could see at least 10 moons! Saturn probably has more than 60 moons, but most of them would be too small to see. Saturn's moons are made up mostly of rock and ice.

New moons are being discovered all the time. Many of them were found during **ring-plane crossings** when it is easier to see what else is **orbiting** Saturn. Many of the others were discovered by **space probes** such as the *Voyagers* and *Cassini*.

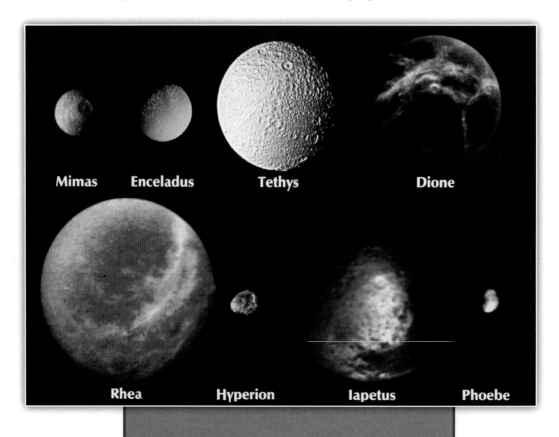

Mimas   Enceladus   Tethys   Dione

Rhea   Hyperion   Iapetus   Phoebe

These are eight of Saturn's many moons.

Titan, the orange moon

Titan is the largest of Saturn's moons and the second largest moon in the **solar system**. It is even bigger than the **planet** Mercury! It was the first of Saturn's moons to be discovered. Titan is the only moon in the solar system that has a **dense** atmosphere. Most of Titan's atmosphere is made up of **nitrogen** gas, just like Earth's atmosphere. Sunlight hitting a small amount of methane in Titan's upper atmosphere makes a thick orange smog. The smog makes the moon look like a smooth orange ball.

Titan is about 1.2 million kilometres (750,000 miles) away from Saturn.

Some of the methane and smog may fall out of the atmosphere like rain. There may be lakes of liquid ethane or methane near the poles. Titan's surface temperature is about −180°C (−290°F). Many scientists think that Titan may be covered with chemicals like the ones on Earth before life began. Titan is about 5,000 kilometres (3,000 miles) wide.

Enceladus, the brightest moon

Enceladus is completely covered by ice. This makes it the brightest **moon** in our **solar system**. Almost all of the sunlight that reaches this moon is reflected. Some scientists think that liquid water and possibly life may exist under the ice. Enceladus is much smaller than the Earth's Moon.

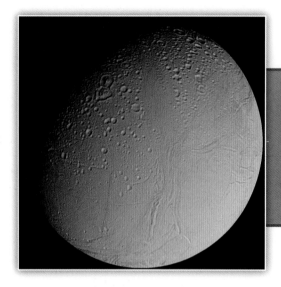

Enceladus is only 500 kilometres (310 miles) wide. It is about 178,000 kilometres (110,600 miles) away from Saturn.

Mimas

Mimas, another of Saturn's moons, is made up almost entirely of frozen water (ice) and is much smaller than Earth's Moon. Long ago a very large object crashed into the surface of Mimas. Scientists think that if the object had been any bigger, it might have broken Mimas into little pieces.

If packed tightly, more than 650 moons the size of Mimas could fit inside Earth's Moon.

In this photo of Saturn, the moon Tethys is above the moon Dione. The shadow of Tethys is near the bottom of the image just below the rings.

Mimas did not break up, but it has the largest **crater** for an object of its size in the entire solar system. The crater is about 130 kilometres (80 miles) across and 10 kilometres (6 miles) deep. If there were a motorway running through the crater, it would take you about one and a half hours to drive from one end to the other.

Does Saturn have any other moons?

Saturn also has some moons that scientists call **shepherd moons**. These moons **orbit** within, or come very close to, Saturn's rings. Any stray ring materials that might otherwise pull away are kept in orbit by these moons. They act like shepherds bringing stray sheep back to the flock. There may be many more shepherd moons that scientists have yet to discover.

What is inside Saturn?

Below the cloud layers of Saturn is a layer of hydrogen gas. Below that is a very deep sea of liquid hydrogen mixed with helium. There is no clear border between the gas in the **atmosphere** and the sea of liquid hydrogen. The two layers of the **planet** blend together.

At the bottom of the liquid layer, the hydrogen is weighed down by all the hydrogen and helium above. The weight makes the hydrogen take on a different form. It acts like a metal that has been melted into a liquid. Scientists call this metallic hydrogen.

Only Saturn's **core**, at the centre of the planet, is solid. Scientists do not know for sure what Saturn's core is made of, but they think it is rock and ice. Saturn's core is about the same size as Earth. The core temperature is about 5,000°C (9,000°F). That is nearly as hot as the surface of the Sun! The icy core can only exist at such high temperatures because the pressure is so strong.

This cutaway drawing of Saturn shows where its different layers start. The layers blend together more than this artwork can show.

Could I ever go to Saturn?

Only if you had a lot of time and money! It takes years to get to Saturn. It would be very expensive to build a spacecraft large enough to hold astronauts and enough food and equipment for such a long journey – and that is just to get there. You would still have to get back to Earth. Communicating with the mission control centre on Earth would also be difficult. It takes more than an hour for a radio signal to travel between Earth and Saturn, even at the speed of light. If there was an emergency and you needed help, the help might arrive too late. Going to Saturn would be difficult and dangerous.

You can look at the pictures, instead

On 1 October 1958, the United States created an organization to study space. They called it the National Aeronautics and Space Administration (NASA). Over time, NASA has become one of the world's leading groups for studying outer space.

This collection of images shows Saturn and eight of its **moons**.

The Pioneer mission to Saturn

In April 1973, NASA sent the *Pioneer 11* **space probe** to study Jupiter and Saturn. In September 1979, *Pioneer 11* flew past Saturn from 20,921 kilometres (13,000 miles) away. It took the first close-up pictures of Saturn. They discovered two new **moons** and another ring, and they found that the moon Titan is too cold to support life.

This is an artist's idea of what it looked like when *Pioneer 11* was reaching Saturn.

The Voyager missions

In 1977, NASA sent two space probes, *Voyager 1* and *Voyager 2*, to study Saturn, Jupiter, Uranus, and Neptune. *Voyager 1* first arrived near Saturn in November 1980. It sent back photos of Saturn's rings. The photos showed that dark, shadowy fingers pointing outwards sometimes form in Saturn's rings. These are called "spokes". Scientists now believe that these spokes are made of clouds of tiny particles that float above the rings. They are shaped by the powerful magnetic field of Saturn.

Where are the Voyagers now?

In 1991 *Voyager 1*'s Saturn mission was complete. It continued on in outer space. Eleven years later, when it was 6 billion kilometres (3.7 billion miles) from the Sun, it sent back a picture of all of the **planets** in the **solar system**. Scientists hope that *Voyager 1* will be able to continue travelling through space in working order until the year 2040. It should continue working until at least 2015.

After visiting Saturn, *Voyager 2* continued on to Uranus and Neptune. More than 20 years after it was launched, *Voyager 2* is still flying through space. Scientists hope that *Voyager 2* will be able to continue working until the year 2034.

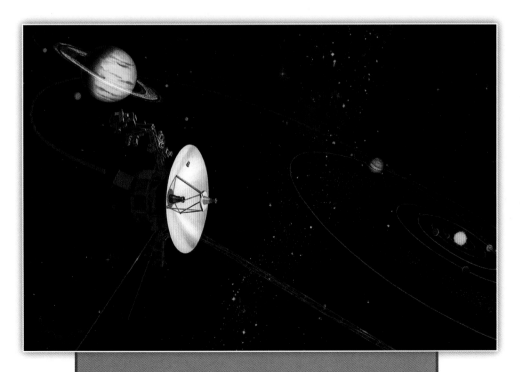

An artist illustrated this vision of what the *Voyager* mission looked like in outer space.

The Cassini mission

In October 1997, NASA launched one of the largest, heaviest **space probes** ever. The *Cassini* mission is expected to last more than 10 years. After flying past Venus and Earth, *Cassini* reached Saturn in July 2004, and has spent the last few years studying Saturn, its rings, and its **moons**. The Italian Space Agency (ASI) and the European Space Agency (ESA) are two of the many groups helping NASA with the project.

The *Cassini* spacecraft has an **orbiter** that has taken many incredible pictures of the moons, rings, and clouds of Saturn. A lot of what we know about Saturn comes from these new images.

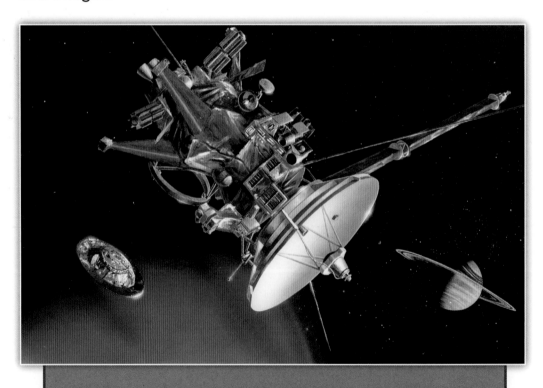

This is an artist's impression of the *Cassini* orbiter as the *Huygens* probe separated from it to enter the atmosphere of Saturn.

The Huygens probe

While exploring Saturn in 2005, NASA's *Cassini* space probe dropped off a European landing craft called *Huygens*. Its heat shield and parachute helped the *Huygens* lander land safely on Titan on 14 January. On its way down through the thick **atmosphere** the lander took hundreds of photographs of what seems to be dry rivers, hills, and sand dunes. Though *Huygens* didn't see any lakes, most scientists think liquid ethane must flow through the dry rivers frequently.

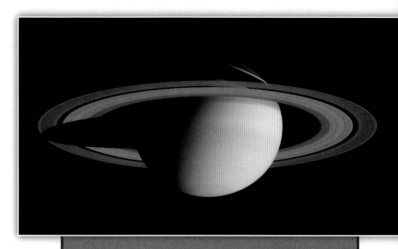

This picture of Saturn was taken by the *Cassini* space probe. The rings cast a shadow on Saturn's northern hemisphere. In the region shadowed by the rings, Saturn's atmosphere has turned a striking blue – perhaps because it is colder there.

What else do we know about the Cassini mission?

- *Cassini* travelled about 3.2 billion kilometres (2 billion miles) just to reach Saturn. This is very far. To travel the same distance, the *Cassini* would have to fly to Earth's Moon and back more than 4,219 times!

- *Cassini* travelled at very fast speeds. At one point, it travelled so fast it was like flying from the west coast to the east coast of the United States in about five minutes!

- On its way to Saturn, *Cassini* "whipped" around Venus twice and around Earth once to use each planet's gravity to build up speed. These **orbits** saved the craft more than 68,040 kilograms (75 tons) of rocket fuel.

Fact File

	SATURN	EARTH
Average distance from the Sun	1,427 million kilometres (887 million miles)	150 million kilometres (93 million miles)
Revolution around the Sun	29.5 Earth **years**	1 Earth year (365 **days**)
Average speed of orbit	9.7 kilometres/second (6.0 miles/second)	30 kilometres/second (18.6 miles/second)
Diameter at equator	120,536 kilometres (74,898 miles)	12 756 kilometres (7,926 miles)
Time for one rotation	10 hours, 39 minutes	24 hours
Atmosphere	hydrogen, helium	oxygen, **nitrogen**
Moons	at least 30	1
Temperature range	–191°C (–312°F) to –69°C (–92°F)	–69°C (–92°F) to 58°C (136°F)

This image shows a lot more detail of the rings of Saturn than many other images of the planet. The shadow of the rings can be seen on the surface of the planet.

A trip to Saturn from Earth

- When Saturn and Earth come closest to each other in their **orbits**, they are 1.28 billion kilometres (793 million miles) apart.

- Travelling to Saturn by car at 113 kilometres (70 miles) per hour would take at least 1,292 years.

- Travelling to Saturn by rocket at 11 kilometres (7 miles) per second would take at least 3 years and 7 months.

More interesting facts:

- Suppose you travelled in a **space probe** from Saturn's inside ring to its outside ring. You would travel more than 273,530 kilometres (170,000 miles) during your trip. To travel this distance on Earth, you would have to fly in a plane almost seven times around Earth.

- Saturn has more **moons** than any other **planet** in our **solar system**. Stray **asteroids** continue to get caught in Saturn's **gravity**, becoming new moons.

- Phoebe, one of Saturn's moons, spins in the opposite direction to all of the other moons of the planet.

Cassini's Gap is in the lower right-hand corner of this image. Colour filters were used to make the rings brighter and easier to see.

Glossary

asteroid large piece of floating rock left over from when the planets formed

astronomer person who studies objects in outer space

atmosphere all of the gases that surround an object in outer space

aurora colourful display caused by charged particles in an atmosphere

axis imaginary line through the middle of an object in space, around which it spins as it rotates

comet ball of ice and rock that orbits around the Sun

core centre of a planet

crater bowl-shaped hole in the ground that is made by a meteorite or a burst of lava

day time it takes for a planet to spin around its axis once

density amount of stuff something is made of compared to how much space it takes up

equator imaginary line around the middle of a planet

gravity invisible force that pulls objects towards the centre of another object in outer space

meteorite piece of rock or dust that lands on the surface of a planet or a moon from space

moon object that floats in an orbit around a planet

nitrogen gas found in the atmosphere of Earth and some of the other planets in our solar system

orbit curved path of one object in space moving around another object

orbiter spacecraft that flies in orbit around a planet

planet large object in space that orbits a central star, has an atmosphere, and does not produce its own light

revolve travel once around the Sun; or, for a moon, to travel once around a planet

ringlet single ring of orbiting dust or ice that combines with other ringlets to form a ring around an object in outer space

ring-plane crossing when all the rings of a planet are lined up to be flat across from a person's point of view

shepherd moons moons in orbit around Saturn's rings that keep material in the rings from breaking out of orbit

solar system group of objects in outer space that all float in orbits around a central star

solar wind material continually coming off of the Sun's surface and travelling through space

space probe craft that carries computers and other instruments to study objects in outer space

star large ball of gas in outer space. A star produces its own light by burning gases.

sulphur yellow-coloured, powdery material. It is found on many planets in gas form.

telescope instrument used by astronomers to study objects in outer space

year time it takes for a planet to orbit the Sun once

More books to read

Exploring Saturn: From Galileo To Cassini, Dan Bortolotti (Firefly Books, 2003)

Out of this World: A Look at Saturn, Ray Spangenburg and Kit Moser (Franklin Watts, 2002)

Stargazers' Guides: Can We Travel to the Stars? Rosalind Mist and Andrew Solway (Heinemann Library, 2006)

Index